MW01046029

# THE GREAT PYRAMID

## ERIK JOHANSEN

P.O. Box 355, Buena Park, CA 90621
www.artesianpress.com

## Nonfiction
## Ancient Egyptian Mystery Series

Cover photo courtesy Steve Underwood
Project Editor: Molly Mraz
Illustrator: Fujiko
Graphic Design: Tony Amaro
©2004 Artesian Press

 *Artesian Press*

ISBN 1-58659-206-8

# CONTENTS

# Word List

**Djoser** (ZHOE-suhr) The Pharaoh who built the first great stone pyramid.

**drought** (drowt) A time when no rain falls and crops are damaged.

**Giza** (GEE-zah) A city in ancient Egypt where the biggest and longest-lasting pyramids are.

**Herodotus** (hih-ROD-uh-tuhs) An ancient Greek writer who wrote about the Great Pyramid.

**Imhotep** (im-HOE-tep) Builder of the greatest mastabas.

**Khufu** (KOO-foo) Sneferu's son and the Pharaoh who built the greatest pyramid of ancient Egypt.

**ma'at** (muh-AHT) The divine order of the universe.

**mastaba** (mahs-TUH-buh) A huge brick building shaped like a rectangle, with a flat top.

**Nile River** (nyuhl) The longest river in the world, found in Egypt.

**papyrus** (puh-PIE-russ) A plant used to make a kind of paper and whose reeds can be woven into a rope.

**Pharaoh** (FARE-oh) Another name for any of the kings who ruled ancient Egypt.

**pi** (pie) The symbol $\pi$. In math it represents the ratio of the circumference of a circle to it diameter.

**Plateau of Giza** (plah-TOE of GEE-zah) A high, flat, wide area of land in Egypt, home of the Great Pyramid of Khufu.

**pyramid** (PEER-uh-mid) A tomb that the ancient Egyptians built for the Pharaoh.

**pyramidion** (peer-uh-MID-ee-on) A stone block covered with sheets of gold that went on top of the pyramid.

**pyramidologist** (peer-uh-mid-AHL-uh-gist) A person who studies pyramids.

**Ra** (rah) The sun god and most important Egyptian god.

**sarcophagus** (sar-COFF-uh-gus) A king's stone coffin.

**Sneferu** (SNEF-uh-roo) The Pharaoh who built the first pyramid.

**zaa** (zah) A group of about a hundred workers.

# Chapter 1

For thousands of years, anyone who has traveled in the Egyptian desert has seen an amazing sight. Most of the desert is nothing but burning-hot sand, but people still come to see the greatest monuments ever built––the pyramids (PEER-uh-midz).

Like a sleeping giant, the largest pyramid rises almost 500 feet above the desert floor. At sunset, it shines golden in the setting sun. The Great Pyramid of Khufu at Giza has stood the test of time. For centuries, the monument has impressed people from all over the world.

The mysteries of the pyramids make us ask many questions. Why were the pyramids built? Who built them? How did each of the heavy stones get put exactly where it belonged? How did the ancient people of Egypt know how to build the pyramids so perfectly, long before modern machines and information? How have the pyramids affected the lives of people to this day? What great secrets have they held for so long—secrets that are just now being discovered? How have the pyramids survived so long while other monuments have disappeared? Will we ever know all the secrets hidden in the pyramids?

To solve some of these mysteries, we need to go back, long before the great pyramids were built.

# Chapter 2

To understand why the pyramids were built, it is important to know what life was like in ancient Egypt. The Great Pyramid of Khufu was built more than 4,000 years ago, but the events leading up to its construction happened long before that.

Because Egypt is mostly desert, water is the most important thing needed for life. The earliest Egyptians built villages near the Nile (NY-uhl) River. The Nile, which is the longest river in the world, was an important reason why the pyramids were built. The Nile runs through Egypt. Because it flows from south to north, the Egyptians called the land in the south

"Upper Egypt," and the land in the north was called "Lower Egypt."

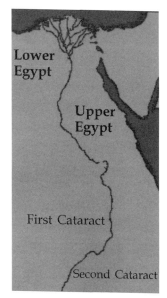

The Nile River carved a narrow green valley in the desert. The first people to live there in ancient times were farmers who grew grain, vegetables, and other food.

Unlike other bodies of water, the Nile flooded the land the same way every season. From June to September, the river flooded, and rich soil from the south filled its waters. When the floodwaters went down, rich new soil was left on the farmland on both sides of the Nile. The farmers were able to grow much-needed food and have a good life. This seasonal flooding made the people think of the world as a dependable and regular place.

The Egyptians began to think of life and the whole universe as a very orderly place. To them, the world was controlled by many gods. The most important god was the sun god, Ra (rah).

Over time, this way of thinking also created a social order in Egypt. The king, who was called the Pharaoh (FAIR-oh), was the most important person in Egyptian society. Egyptians believed the Pharaoh was put on the earth by the gods to keep what they called *ma'at* (muh-AHT), which means the divine order of the universe. The people obeyed the Pharaoh and honored him by giving him their crops and other belongings. The Pharaoh's job was to keep the Nile flooding so that there was plenty of food and the people were happy.

In the social order of Egypt, the

Pharaoh and his high officials were at the top and had the most power. After them came lower officials, priests, craftsmen, town leaders, and rich farmers. The majority of the rest of the people were mostly small farmers.

Because the Egyptians believed their Pharaoh got his power from the gods, his death was a very important event in all their lives. They did everything possible to make sure his spirit would be safe and would live with the other gods in the afterlife. His funeral and the placing of his body in his own pyramid became the most important event in the lives of the Egyptians.

A pyramid was built as a huge tomb to house the dead body of the Pharaoh, along with all the things he would need for his journey to the afterlife. According to ancient writings, the Egyptians believed that when their Pharaoh died, the sun would send its beams to the earth and make a golden ramp to the heavens. The Pharaoh's spirit would then travel up the ramp and meet with Ra every morning at sunrise. This explains why the pyramid's four sides all point to the heavens. They symbolized the ramps the Pharaoh used to meet with Ra.

*How* the pyramids were made was one of the great mysteries of ancient Egypt. Many questions about this mystery kept experts wondering for a very long time. For instance, how could an ancient people make such a perfect building without using modern technology? Where did they get their information? Why did the Egyptians stop building pyramids if they were so important to them? Most interesting of all, how did the pyramids get the strange shape that made them so famous? Finding these answers would solve one of the greatest mysteries of all time.

# Chapter 3

There are more than eighty pyramids scattered across Egypt. The three at the Plateau of Giza (plah-TOE of GEE-zah) are the longest-lasting and largest ones ever built. The largest of the three is the Great Pyramid of Khufu. To many people, it is the greatest monument of all time.

Part of the answer to the question of how it was built is the huge number of people who worked on it. Over time, a working system was organized based on the flooding season of the Nile. This system let farmers grow their crops during part of the year and spend the rest of their time working on the pyramids. Fishermen, hunters, and others also worked on the pyramids according to the seasons of the Nile.

Most Egyptians worked on this pyramid. This large group of workers was very well organized. Experts used to think the workers were mostly slaves. They later learned that the workers were not slaves and were well fed and well treated. They probably did the work as a religious service to the gods and Pharaoh who they believed ruled the universe. As long as the people thought their leader was the reason they had such a good life, they wanted to help him in every way possible--even after he died. That way, he could continue to help them from the next life.

What puzzled experts for hundreds of years was how the pyramids were built without any similar buildings being built before them as examples. Most historical events of this kind change slowly by "trial and error." That means that a way of doing something is tried, and if it works, it is used again. If it does not work, people learn from the mistake and try something different.

At first, experts did not see examples of trial and error in the building of the pyramids. It seemed as though the pyramids suddenly appeared, perfectly built, and then stopped being built all of a sudden. However, over time, the experts did find examples of earlier efforts at pyramid building that prove the trial-and-error method was used.

The earliest-known examples of pyramids were called mastabas (muh-STAH-buhs). *Mastaba* is an Arabic word that means "bench." They were huge, flat-topped buildings made of mud bricks and shaped like long rectangles.

A builder named Imhotep (ihm-HOE-tep) created the best design for these mastabas. Imhotep was so admired for his skill, he became the only non-royal Egyptian to be worshipped like a god. About 4,700 years ago, he built the grandest mastaba of all.

Imhotep designed this grand mastaba during the rule of Pharaoh Djoser (ZHOE-suhr). For the first time, a building was made of stone instead of brick. It looked as if several mastabas were piled on top of each other.

Fifty years later, Pharaoh Sneferu (SNEF-uh-roo) ordered that an eight-step mastaba be built. It was stopped when Sneferu changed his mind and

©Steve Underwood

*Djoser's step pyramid looked like many mastabas stacked on top of each other.*

decided the huge mastaba should have smooth sides. The eight-step mastaba was never finished.

When the smooth-sided mastaba was about half built, a major problem was found. The sides of the mastaba began to fall because they were too steep. Instead of giving up completely, they made a change in the design. Sneferu's change in the angle caused a bend in the middle of the building that can still be seen today.

Sneferu then ordered another building to be built near the last one. Since the ancient Egyptians learned from their mistakes, this new building was built with smooth sides and stood at a perfect angle. It is the earliest-known example of a true pyramid.

Sneferu's son, Khufu (KOO-foo), learned a lot from his father. By the time Khufu ruled Egypt, his pyramid became the greatest ever. It became the symbol of Egypt for all time.

# Chapter 4

The pyramids at Giza (GEE-zah) are one of the Seven Wonders of the Ancient World. They are the only Wonder that is still standing. The Great Pyramid of Khufu is the largest of the three. It stands nearly 500 feet high, as tall as a thirty-nine-story building. Its four sides have an average length of 756 feet. The north side faces true north and is only off by one-tenth of a degree. It was built with 2 million heavy limestone blocks, each block weighing at least 2 tons.

It is hard for experts to explain these amazing facts about such an ancient building. How was such a huge creation made without modern tools

*The pyramids of Giza are the only one of the Seven Wonders of the Ancient World still standing.*

and skills? We still don't know everything about the pyramids, but we have learned much from research.

In the fifth century B.C., the Greek writer Herodotus (hih-ROD-uh-tuhs) visited the Great Pyramid of Khufu. Herodotus heard amazing tales. He was even told that machines lifted the heavy stones! Historians argued about what Herodotus wrote, which caused even more questions about the building of the pyramids. The mystery is only now beginning to be solved. Recent experiments and new findings have uncovered many more clues.

The pyramid builders learned many ways to make the process easier and faster. The Egyptian workforce, engineers, and officials all became experts at building pyramids by the time Khufu's pyramid was built.

How many people helped, and how long did it take them to build the Great Pyramid? One scientist figured that in order to finish the pyramid in twenty years (about the time that Khufu ruled Egypt), the Egyptian builders needed to put about 340 blocks in place each day. Since a workday lasted about ten hours, they set thirty-four blocks every hour!

After his visit to ancient Egypt, Herodotus wrote that more than 100,000 workers helped build the pyramid. Recent studies, however, think that he counted the number of people who worked on the pyramid during an entire year. Probably only

25,000 workers spent three months at a time at the pyramid. That means there were 100,000 workers a year.

Workers were grouped into crews of about two thousand men, then split up into two gangs of one thousand workers. The gangs were separated into five groups called *zaas* (zahz), which had about two hundred men each. Each zaa had ten divisions of twenty men.

The gangs all had different names. They combined the king's name and other words to make names such as Friends of Khufu. The five zaas always had the same names: the Great (or Right Side), the Asiatic (or Left Side), the Green (or Front), the Little (or Back), and the Last (or Good) Zaa.

Building the Great Pyramid made Egypt one of the greatest nations of ancient times. We can see how this happened by looking at the way Egyptian life was organized at the time.

# Chapter 5

The pyramids were very important monuments to the Pharaohs of Egypt. During the Age of Pyramids, Egypt began to grow along the banks of the Nile River.

Population grew around the building of a pyramid. The Pharaoh built a large home close to the pyramid. From his home, he watched over the project. Farmers, bakers, brewers, and craftsmen lived nearby to support the Pharaoh and the pyramid builders. Priests and officials also lived near the pyramid work. The thousands of people who actually worked on the pyramid needed to live close to the job, too.

One Egyptian temple, much smaller

*Egyptians built pyramids near the Nile River.*

than Khufu's Great Pyramid, has this list of products used in just one year while the temple was being built:

>100,800 servings of beer and cake
>
>7,720 loaves of bread
>
>1,002 oxen
>
>1,000 geese

Imagine what the list might look like for the crews of Khufu's Pyramid!

Someone needed to transport and store all these products. Then a system was organized to make sure all of the food and materials got to the builders.

That meant a town needed to be built next to each pyramid. Large temporary villages for the workforce were also built.

Each pyramid had a royal palace where the Pharaoh stayed when he lived near the pyramid. These large houses and the grounds around the palace needed many workers. According to paintings in one of the pyramids on the Plateau of Giza, its palace included:

    2 managers of the estate
    11 scribes (people who could write) who recorded the history and business of the estate
    1 manager of the workforce
    2 managers of the dining hall
    2 managers of the house linen
    1 seal carrier (the man who carried and used the mark of the Pharaoh)
    3 meat cutters

2 bakers

1 cook

5 head servants

These people worked and lived in the household. Around the outside of the palace, there were smaller houses where the workers lived. High priests and officials lived in the larger houses.

Farther away from the main palace, there were hundreds of small houses where the other workers lived. After the Pharaoh died and was buried in the pyramid, even smaller mud houses began to appear closer to the pyramid and around the palace. These houses were built in a very disorganized way.

Some very recent discoveries make it clear that the Egyptian workers ate bread and drank an early form of beer. There are also signs that they ate a lot of fish. When the Nile River Valley flooded each year, it created some large lakes that were perfect for raising catfish. Each year, catfish entered the valley from the river, providing a huge "fish market" to help the Pharaoh feed his workers.

The bread the workers ate was baked in clay pots. The wheat they used was different from the wheat we use to make bread today. Ancient Egyptian bread was very heavy. One loaf was enough to feed one person for several days.

All of the teamwork needed to build the pyramids also helped to organize and make Egypt into a great nation. With a better understanding of the workforce and what the workers did, the next mystery was one of the hardest to figure out. *How* did they do it? What tools did they use to build the pyramids? These are questions experts are still trying to answer today.

# Chapter 6

The Egyptians used simple tools to build the pyramids. One tool, called a plumb bob, was a string with a weight that hung straight down to measure straight lines. They also used different lengths of string and rope to help them measure.

They also used wooden squares to measure corners. They also used many types of tools to cut and shape stones. It is hard to believe the Egyptians were able to build such perfectly shaped buildings with such simple tools!

The Egyptian builders created a level base for the pyramids by using simple wooden devices. To measure whether the surface was truly level, some people think that they put water on the surface to see if it would run off. It is more likely that they used an A-shaped wooden frame with a plumb bob string suspended from the top of the "A" on the frame. When the string hung straight across a mark made on the crosspiece of the "A," the surface was then level.

©Fujiko

*Ancient Egyptians used wooden squares and A-frame levels with plumb bobs to build the pyramids.*

The pyramid builders ran into trouble when they tried to cut the large stones so they would fit together. They had to drill holes into the stones to break them. They also needed to saw large sections of stone. This was difficult because the Egyptians did not yet know about iron and steel. They used copper saws, but copper is softer than some of the stone they needed to cut. So they put a mixture of water and sharp, tiny, harder stones into the cut. The copper tool helped to push and pull these hard, sharp pieces into the stone to cut it.

The builders created the smooth finish on the surface of the completed pyramids using very small chisels. The chisels were only a third of an inch wide—not much wider than a pencil. They also made the chisels out of soft copper, so they had to sharpen them very often. Archeologists figured the Egyptians needed one full-time chisel sharpener for each one hundred chiselers. Thousands of chiselers worked on the pyramids at a time.

To pound and break stones, the builders used other stones that were much harder. These stones weighed between 9 and 15 pounds each. The builders had to use both hands to use the stones like hammers. Hammers of today usually weigh a little over one pound. Egyptian stone pounders had to be very strong.

How did the Egyptians get the stones to the pyramid site? How did they ever lift stones that were as heavy as an average car to the height needed to build a pyramid and then put them in place? Experts are still arguing over the answers to these questions.

©National Museum of Scotland

*Pounders (left) and chiselers (right) worked on the pyramid.*

# Chapter 7

Experts disagree on some of the details, but we now know much more about how the ancient Egyptians built the pyramids. Most experts agree that they used boats, ramps, rollers, sleds, ropes, and pulleys.

There is a saying that "the best way to do a difficult task is to find the easy way to do it." Building the pyramids was hard work, but the Egyptians found easier ways to do it.

The rocky mountains where the stones were cut were not near the pyramids. Once the stones were cut, how did they get them onto the boats and then move them from the boats to the pyramid? In some cases, it was simply a matter of tumbling the stones very carefully. Twenty men pulled the stones with heavy ropes made from papyrus (puh-PIE-russ) reeds. Two men in the back would steer the stone, using long poles as levers. This moved the stones from where they were cut to the banks of the Nile River. Then, very carefully, they were loaded onto boats.

Why did they use boats? It would have taken many men a long time to carry the huge stones to the pyramid. Instead, the Egyptians let the Nile River do some of the work for them. They

*Egyptians used cargo ships like this one to carry stones to the pyramid.*

floated the stones down the Nile until they got close to the pyramid.

Using levers, they carefully unloaded the stones from the boats and put them on specially built sleds. These sleds were then pulled along wet and slippery clay tracks that led to the pyramid. Archeologists have found some of these tracks and sleds near the pyramid site.

Ancient ramps made of dirt and sand have also been found near the pyramids. The ramps show how the Egyptians raised the stones above ground level. However, once the pyramid began to get higher and higher, how were the heavy stones raised to each new higher level?

Since ramps became very dangerous at the higher levels of the pyramid, the Egyptians raised the giant stones a different way. Strange, mushroom-shaped stones have been found near the pyramids. Experts believe that these stones are the earliest version of a pulley. Raised up on ramps, the pulleys had very strong ropes running through them. A hundred workers pulled these ropes to raise the stones. The pulleys also helped keep the rope from wearing out, as it would have if it were dragged along the side of the pyramid. Placing the stones was still dangerous, but with practice, the workers became skilled at the job.

The hardest and most dangerous work of all was yet to come. Experts now believe that the top of a pyramid had a sort of capstone, which the ancient Egyptians called a *pyramidion* (peer-uh-MID-ee-uhn). It was a single, pyramid-shaped block of stone that was covered with sheets of gold. It was made to reflect the rising or setting sun while everything else below was in shadow. This was done so that the dead Pharaoh would have a ramp to the sun for his journey to the afterlife.

How did such a heavy object get to the top of the very steep pyramid?

It is generally believed that the pyramidion was put in place by workers who picked it up and then ran to the top of the pyramid! Can you imagine a handful of specially trained men running upward from the pyramid's highest ramp while carrying the heavy pyramidion and then placing it on the top? The other workers must have held their breath as the men raced to the very top of the pyramid. If even one of these men made a mistake, the result would have been a disaster.

Paintings have survived that show the workers had a big party after the pyramidion was successfully placed. The pyramid was then finished!

# Chapter 8

The inside of the Great Pyramid of Khufu is the most complex of all the pyramids. It contains many levels and amazing rooms. There is an upward passageway that leads to a beautiful granite hall called the Grand Gallery. It leads to the main burial room of the king. In earlier pyramids, the king's chamber was at ground level or lower.

The entrance to the inside is on the north face of the pyramid, about 55 feet above the ground. Builders sealed the entrance with a swivel door made of a stone that weighed 20 tons. That is about as heavy as two huge male elephants! It took very little effort to push the door open from the inside.

When the door was closed, however, the fit was so perfect that it was almost impossible to see it from the outside.

The main entrance leads to a downward passage. It goes through the inside of the pyramid and ends in a room called the Subterranean Chamber, which means "underground room." This passage is about 345 feet long. It ends 98 feet below the ground in the small chamber.

About 60 feet from the pyramid entrance, there is a hole in the stone roof that leads to another passageway. This is the entrance to the upward passageway that leads to the Grand Gallery and the King's Chamber. It is 129 feet long and goes up into the middle of the pyramid. The original entrance to this passage was blocked by three very heavy stones, which are still in place. Some men (probably grave robbers) tried to enter the tomb long after the pyramid was sealed. They made a hole in the roof of the downward passage so they could get around these large stones.

The upward passage leads to the Grand Gallery. It is also made with very heavy stones. Four large, hollow stones support the walls of this hall.

At the beginning of the Grand Gallery is a flat passage that leads to another room. Arab explorers thought the queen was buried in this room, so they named it the Queen's Chamber. However, there is no proof that it actually was for a queen. The Egyptians probably built this room for a statue of the king. Other pyramids built earlier or at the same time had similar rooms that were used for statues. This room is located exactly on the centerline that runs from east to west through the pyramid.

In the walls there are also small openings that lead to small shafts. These shafts end deep inside the pyramid. People thought that they were never finished or that they were used as air passages. A more recent belief is that these shafts point to certain stars. The ancient Egyptians may have made the shafts as a sort of "spirit exit" for the Pharaoh's soul.

At the south end of the Grand Gallery, there is an entrance that leads to an antechamber, which is like a small room or short hallway. The antechamber protects the entrance to the king's tomb.

Inside the antechamber were three huge flat stones in the ceiling. The stones were placed one behind the other. When King Khufu's coffin was placed inside the pyramid, the tomb was sealed with these large stones. When the priests left the main room, they knocked out the wood beams that were holding up the stones. Then the stones slid down three slots in the walls of the antechamber, closing the tomb forever! They probably got out of the sealed antechamber through the very narrow shaft that leads to the downward passageway. They sealed this small passageway with a stone that was cut so exactly, it was almost impossible to see the opening. That made it difficult for outsiders to enter the king's tomb.

The King's tomb is the main room in the pyramid and is called the King's Chamber. It is made of beautiful pink-colored stone called rose granite. It is located on the fiftieth row of stones inside the pyramid. The stones used for this room are the heaviest in the entire pyramid. They fit together so perfectly, a baseball card cannot even fit between them.

The king's granite coffin is called a *sarcophagus* (sar-COFF-uh-gus) and is in this room. It is placed in the room so that its sides line up perfectly with the points of the compass: north, south, east, and west. The sarcophagus is too big to fit in the passageway. The workers probably put it inside before they finished the chamber, while the pyramid was still open at the top. The builders carved the coffin, which weighs about 3 tons, from a single block of rose granite.

The lid of the sarcophagus is missing. Thieves probably broke it when they opened the coffin. Experts think even the lid weighed more than 2 tons.

Above the King's Chamber is a series of five smaller chambers. They are called the Relieving Chambers and were built to help spread out the weight of the heavy stones. Perhaps the Egyptians learned from earlier pyramids that chamber roofs needed to be light so they would not cave in.

At the top of the highest chamber are two stones in the shape of a roof. These stones also helped to spread the weight of the pyramid away from the King's Chamber. This was the first time the pyramid designers used this idea.

When explorers opened the five Relieving Chambers, everyone who entered the second chamber turned black from a powder that was found only in that chamber. When scientists studied the powder, they found that it was made of the shells and skins of dead insects from long ago.

The walls of the Relieving Chambers are the only place in the pyramid where there is writing. Workers didn't think anyone would ever see these walls. They wrote that they were the workers of Khufu, so we know that this pyramid was his tomb.

Workers sealed the main entrance of the pyramid with limestone to try to hide the pyramid's entrance.

Only one part of the Great Pyramid is still unexplored. The shafts in the

Grand Gallery mentioned earlier are areas no one has ever seen. In 1993, German scientists built a tiny robot to explore the narrow shafts and discover more about these last unknown areas of the Great Pyramid. Experts believe that these passages were meant to be used by the Pharaoh's spirit because they are aimed at special stars in the sky. The robot was fitted with a special camera and traveled 213 feet along one of the shafts. When it came to a small door, it could go no further. The pictures from the camera show a mysterious goo oozing from the edges of the door.

Why was the door placed in the shaft? What lies beyond this tiny door? What is the strange goo? The modern Egyptian government has not yet allowed the research to continue. What lies beyond the tiny door is still a mystery.

# Chapter 9

There are other interesting facts about the pyramids besides how they were built. The Egyptians did an amazing job of building the pyramids so that they lined up directly with the stars. Each side of the pyramids at Giza points to one of the four points of the compass: north, south, east, and west. That is a very difficult task.

The three major pyramids at Giza are placed in the same pattern as three stars in the sky called Orion's Belt, which is part of the constellation Orion (oh-RI-uhn) the Hunter. This was the way Egyptian architects did things at that time. The pyramids often mirrored the location of the stars in the heavens.

The pyramids were used as a sundial, an early clock that can tell time by the movement of an object's shadow based on the position of the

*Orion the Hunter affected how the pyramids were built.*

sun. This is a very useful tool in a land where the sun shines brightly almost every day.

With the angle of its sides and its placement on the earth, the Great Pyramid casts no shadow at noon on the first day of spring. This makes the Great Pyramid's location a very special place on the earth. How were the Egyptians able to be so exact?

There are two basic ideas about how the pyramids were placed with such skill. Some experts believe the builders used the stars to figure out which direction was north. One archeologist demonstrated this idea. He built a wall in the shape of a circle, just high enough so a person could only see the night sky from inside the wall. The wall was perfectly level and straight. It acted as a level line. A person stood in the exact center of the circle at night and watched each star move above the horizon. A point was marked on the wall to show the place where the star rose. Another mark was made at the point where the star set. The middle point of those two marks stood for due north.

Another way the ancient Egyptians may have found north was by using the points where the sun rises and sets each day. This idea makes sense because the Egyptians worshipped the sun god, Ra. Whatever method the Egyptians used, they were very accurate in their measurements.

Before the Great Pyramid was built, the Egyptians did not line up any other pyramid as carefully as Khufu's. The Great Pyramid's measurements present some interesting facts. Some say that the length of the pyramid's sides is mathematically related to the number of days in a year. There is also a slight curve designed into the four sides of the pyramid. People believe this curve exactly matches the curve of the earth's surface! However, the Great Pyramid is very old and exact measurements of its sides are difficult to figure out today.

Another question that still puzzles experts is if the pyramids were built as burial chambers, why is it that not a single buried king has been found? Some people believe grave robbers are the reason. Another reason is that perhaps the *real* burial place of Khufu has not yet been found. Some things about the pyramids might remain mysteries for all time because that's exactly what the Egyptians wanted.

# Chapter 10

Why did the Egyptians stop building pyramids? The answer has to do with several things that began to change the lives of the ancient Egyptians.

To better understand what happened in ancient Egypt, historians have divided its history into Old, Middle, and New Kingdoms. These kingdoms were marked by great moments in Egyptian history. Historians call the time between these kingdoms "lesser periods." These were the times in Egyptian history when bad things happened, such as a decline in the great country's culture and the weakening of its central power.

There was a big change in the climate, called a drought (drowt), about 4,000 years ago. It lasted a long time. The Nile River stopped flooding regularly. This ended the Old Kingdom and began a time when Pharaohs were weak but local rulers were strong. This meant the power of Egypt was no longer in the control of the main government but was divided among smaller rulers.

The drought of the Nile created widespread hunger. Sometimes the local rulers could feed the people and the Pharaohs could not. This showed the people that the Pharaohs were *not* gods. The people saw that the Pharaohs were unable to keep the Nile flowing and flooding.

During the bad times at the end of the Old Kingdom, other countries tried to invade Egypt. Sometimes they were successful. There was also war between the local rulers.

Egypt was no longer the country it once was. Pharaohs were no longer believed to be human gods. The country changed, and hunger was everywhere. Over time, all of these things helped to bring a sad end to the amazing age of great pyramid building.

When the climate improved again, the power of a united Egypt returned. It was the beginning of the Middle Kingdom. However, by this time, the thinking changed in many ways. The pyramids were not thought to be safe burial places because of grave robbers. Pyramids also became too expensive to build. The Pharaohs were no longer believed to be gods in the way they were in the past. The people's faith in the Pharaohs did not completely return until the New Kingdom.

The age of the large pyramids ended. Would the great monuments survive the test of time?

# Chapter 11

Over time, many amazing stories have been told about the pyramids. As people from different parts of the world looked at the giant buildings, the legend of the pyramids grew in very strange ways.

Even though the Greek writer Herodotus was impressed by what he saw, the ancient Romans were not. When the Romans first saw the monuments, they thought they were a foolish waste of time and energy. Some Romans decided the only reason the pyramids were built was so the Pharaoh would be able to selfishly use all his treasures during his lifetime. The Romans believed he did not want to leave behind anything of value for future Pharaohs.

During the Middle Ages, even more amazing stories were told. A popular belief was that the pyramids were huge storage buildings for grain. People thought that the pyramids were built during the biblical time of Joseph, when there was a famine for seven years.

Muslim Arabs probably changed their opinion about the pyramids more than anybody else. At first, the Arabs thought the pyramids were like libraries. They believed all the wisdom of a great ancient people was stored inside the buildings.

However, around the time of the Middle Ages, Muslim leaders had a different opinion about the pyramids. Muslim rulers ordered that the pyramids be stripped of their smooth, outer white stones. The white limestone was then used to build houses and bridges in Cairo, the modern Egyptian capital.

In the 1800s, a Muslim ruler named Mohammed Ali wanted to go even further. If the outer limestone could be used to make houses, then he wanted to take apart the Great Pyramid completely. If this had happened, the hard work of the ancient Egyptians would have been used to build houses for the Muslim leader and his people.

Ali was about to order this destruction when he received new information. A place closer to Cairo had stones that could be cut out of the ground more easily than breaking apart the Great Pyramid. Ali changed his mind, and the Great Pyramid barely escaped being leveled to the ground.

In later years, other people began to discover different things about the pyramids. In the 1860s, a British magazine writer, John Taylor, became very interested in the pyramids. He read all that he could about them and made some new findings. He discovered that if he added the length of two of the pyramid's sides and then divided that number by the pyramid's height, the answer would be very close to the value of pi (pie), a number that describes the measurement of a circle.

It was thought that pi was discovered in the sixth century by a Hindu mathematician. What was so amazing is that John Taylor's claim meant the ancient Egyptians figured it out several thousand years *before* that!

Taylor continued his study of the pyramids until his death in 1864. Many people made fun of him, but some now say a Scottish astronomer, Charles Smyth, proved Taylor's discoveries were correct.

Soon, the Great Pyramid was believed to hold all the wisdom of the ages. Some people made their own discoveries and really believed what they found. They thought that the

Great Pyramid could explain when the world was created. Some people even believed it gave the exact day and time the world would *end*. These people believed the world would end on the longest day of the year in 2045. Of course, they had many critics who did not believe them. The people who studied the pyramids to learn about the world called themselves *pyramidologists* (peer-uh-mid-AHL-uh-gists). Those who did not believe what the pyramidologists found called them *pyramidiots*.

Because the pyramids were built with such advanced information, some people believed that aliens from another planet helped the ancient Egyptians build them. They believed that after the pyramids were completed, the aliens returned to their own planet and took their wisdom with them.

The theory that aliens helped the ancient Egyptians came from a very popular book of the 1960s called *Chariot of the Gods*. The author believed aliens must have helped them because the information used to build the pyramids was far more advanced than what he believed the Egyptians knew at the time. He didn't give much credit to the clever ancient Egyptians.

Not many experts believed the theories in *Chariot of the Gods*. They considered them too strange to be true, like the legend of Bigfoot or the Loch Ness Monster. However, this did not stop some pyramidologists from continuing their studies.

In the twentieth century, many people all over the world believed the pyramids held special powers. Models were made and used for everything from growing crops to healing the sick. To this day, some people believe the pyramids have a sort of magical power. The fact is, they are amazing structures that have stood the test of time.

# Chapter 12

Today, the three pyramids on the Giza Plateau are among the most famous tourist attractions in the world. Visitors come from everywhere to marvel at their incredible size and perfection.

Visitors can see the beauty of the pyramids in the daytime. At night, an amazing laser-light show makes the pyramids come to life in the darkness. Visitors can go inside the Great Pyramid to see the two passageways, the Subterranean Chamber, the Great Gallery, the Queen's Chamber, and, of course, the King's Chamber.

The shape of the Great Pyramid of Khufu has inspired builders throughout the centuries. Romans used the shape as tombs in their cemeteries. Artists admired the simple, beautiful form of the pyramid and used it in their work.

After Napoleon visited Egypt in 1798, more pyramids appeared in European buildings. By the 1800s, many designers in Europe used pyramids in houses, parks, bridges, and gardens. Pyramids also became popular grave markers in Europe.

Today the pyramid is still a very popular form. You can see a large skyscraper in the shape of a pyramid from miles away in San Francisco, California. The most famous art museum in France, the Louvre, has a large glass pyramid as part of its entrance. The Luxor Hotel in Las Vegas, Nevada, is a very large pyramid designed to look like the Great Pyramid of Khufu in Egypt. The back of the U.S. one-dollar bill has a pyramid with an eye at its top. California State

*The basketball stadium at California State University, Long Beach, is shaped like a pyramid.*

University of Long Beach is famous for its basketball stadium that is shaped like a giant pyramid.

The pyramid's shape—square on the bottom with triangle-shaped sides pointing to the heavens at the top—continues to inspire people everywhere. They still amaze people today who see them as great monuments to the Pharaohs and people of Egypt. The old Arab proverb may be true: "Man fears Time, yet Time fears the Pyramids."

# Bibliography

Berg, Christopher. *Amazing Art: Wonders of the Ancient World*. New York: Harper Resource, 2001.

Bulliet, Richard, et. al. *The Earth and Its Peoples: A Global History*, 3d ed. Boston: Houghton-Mifflin, 2001.

Chisholm, Jane, and Anne Millard, eds. *The Usborne Book of the Ancient World: Early Civilization*. Tulsa, Okla.: EDC Publishing, 1998.

Crystal, Ellie. *Crystalinks*. Internet Web site: www.crystalinks.com (1995)

Fink, N. A. *Explore Ancient Egypt's Pyramids*. Internet Web site: www.guardians.net (2000)

Innes, Brian. *Unsolved Mysteries: Mysteries of the Ancients*. Austin, Tex.: Steck-Vaughn, 1999.

James, Peter, and Nick Thorp. *Ancient Mysteries.* New York: Ballantine, 1999.

Lehner, Mark. *The Complete Pyramids.* London: Thames & Hudson, 1997.

Morris, Margaret. *The Egyptian Pyramid Mystery Is Solved!* Internet Web site: www.margaretmorrisbooks.com (2001)

# Other Nonfiction Read-Alongs

## Disasters

- Challenger
- The Kuwaiti Oil Fires
- The Last Flight of 007
- The Mount St. Helens Volcano
- The Nuclear Disaster at Chernobyl

Disaster Display Set (5 each of 5 titles 25 books in all)
80106

## Natural Disasters

- Blizzards
- Earthquakes
- Hurricanes and Floods
- Tornadoes
- Wildfires

Disaster Display Set (5 each of 5 titles 25 books in all)
80032

**www.artesianpress.com**